THE SPUR BOOK
of
WALKING

Also in this series of
VENTURE GUIDES:

THE SPUR BOOK
of
WALKING

by
Rob Hunter

SPURBOOKS LIMITED

Published 1978 by:
SPURBOOKS LTD.
6 Parade Court
Bourne End
Bucks

The author and publishers would like to thank Ray Jones of the YHA, London, Jes Miller of Jeans, St. Albans, Eric Gurney of the Backpackers Club, Tony Lack of Pindisports, and John Merrill, for their help and advice in the preparation of this book.

ISBN 0 904978 91 5

Printed by Maund & Irvine, Ltd., Tring, Herts.

CONTENTS

INTRODUCTION

ABOUT THIS SERIES

Venture Guides are written for the guidance and instruction of all those who enjoy active leisure pursuits, and they fall into two broad areas.

The first group covers such basic but essential outdoor skills as Knot-tying, Map reading and Compass work, Camping and Cooking skills, Weather Lore, First Aid, and Survival and Rescue techniques. These are the skills which all outdoor people should possess. A full list of such titles will be found in the front of this book.

The second group covers what we describe as Venture Sports. These are activities which do not require mechanical assistance and are not team games. This group therefore includes such activities as Rock Climbing, Hill Trekking, Backpacking, Snorkelling, Sailing, Downhill and Cross-Country Ski-ing, and Canoeing, and again, a list is at the front of the book.

To this second group we now add this book, an introductory guide to the fascinating pastime of walking and rambling, which will, we hope, convert many casual strollers into country walkers.

ABOUT THIS BOOK

On the face of it nothing could be more straightforward than walking. You put one foot in front of another and away you go. That will get you round the garden or the local park, but if you want to travel further, over country tracks and footpaths, in fair weather and foul, then you need a certain amount of equipment and know-how. Such finer matters are the subject of this book.

In recent years, all outdoor activities have expanded tremendously, with millions of people out every weekend, trekking across the countryside in organised groups or family parties. Walking is the most innocent and harmless of pastimes, but if ramblers enter the countryside in such large numbers, then certain conventions must be known and observed, or the peace and quiet they seek will be rapidly eroded, quite apart from the pressure their presence exerts on the farming community and wildlife.

Moreover, walking is a means to an end as well as an end in itself. The feet can propel you virtually anywhere, into extreme conditions, and remote country. As this happens, further equipment, experience, and help is often necessary. You can start on the local footpaths and end up anywhere. Just take it — like walking — a step at a time.

Chapter 1

THE FOOTPATH NETWORK

The basis of rambling in the U.K. and the Continent is the footpath network, a system of tracks, roads and greenways, handed down to us from time immemorial.

They are, quite literally, a priceless heritage dating back in some instances to prehistoric times. In Britain the Ridgeway and Icknield Way date back certainly to the late Stone Age, while Offa's Dyke was built by King Offa of Mercia, to protect his Kingdom from the rampaging Welsh long before the Conquest. In France, the Grande Randonnée (GR65) from Le Puy to Toulouse, marks the medieval pilgrim track across France to Compostella in Spain, while back in England we have our own Pilgrim's Way running from Winchester to the shrine of St. Thomas at Canterbury, a historic track and the basis of the Canterbury Tales.

The bulk of our local footpaths were established as common rights-of-way in the time of the Saxons. "Three times make the custom" as the old folk said, and the web of footpaths today often link up points which are today of only historical importance, marking parish boundaries, routes to church or chapel, or finishing fortuitously in the village inn. It is custom, rather than law, which established the footpath networks, in a period long before walking for pleasure was imagined, let along practiced, and the law says that twenty years of free walking establishes a path as a right-of-way. The responsibility for maintaining footpaths rests with your local County Council, which may explain why some five hundred miles of footpath vanish every year.

RIGHTS-OF-WAY

A public footpath or bridleway is a "right-of-way". In the case of a footpath, it is open to pedestrians only, while bridleways are for walkers and people on horseback. Both exclude wheeled vehicles other than bicycles.

It has to be faced that the walker and the country community are frequently at loggerheads over rights-of-way and the law is explicit in general, but vague in practice.

A 'right-of-way' is just that. It permits anyone to cross a farm or private property provided he or she sticks to the established route and does no damage on the way. Lighting fires, scaring cattle, letting a dog chase sheep, trampling standing crops, tumbling down stone walls, leaving gates open, or leaving tins or plastic bags to damage the livestock or for cows to eat, are not included in the 'right' and yet is is just this sort of bad behaviour which upsets the country community and all too often leads to retaliation when footpaths are ploughed up or wired off. Walls and fences can appear across routes, while a decidedly surly welcome, of the "git orf moi land" variety, is liable to take the joy out of the walker's day.

This said, by and large, relations between walkers and farmers are generally good. There is no need for any townie making his lawful way across the land to quail when an honest rustic hoves into sight. The farmers realise that having a large number of ramblers on their side as country lovers can be useful when the planners and bureaucrats decide to launch yet another motorway or development across their land, and while their 'rights' often conflict, their aims are basically the same.

Live and let live is the way to get along together, and the best way to ensure that this fragile amity continues and expands, is to observe the Country Code, a list of precepts laid down for all who go into the countryside.

THE COUNTRY CODE
1. Guard against all risks of fire.
2. Fasten all gates.
3. Keep dogs under proper control.
4. Keep to the paths across farmland.
5. Avoid damaging fences, hedges and walls.
6. Leave no litter.
7. Safeguard water supplies.
8. Protect wildlife, wild plants and trees.
9. Go carefully on country roads.
10. Respect the life of the countryside.

WAYMARKING
Not all footpaths are signposted or 'waymarked'. The waymark can be a signpost, an arrow in a tree, or a little symbol like an acorn sign.

All footpaths *should* be waymarked, and the Countryside Commission are trying to introduce standard waymarks of yellow arrows on footpaths and blue arrows on bridleways.

In France, the Grande Randonnée is indicated by red and white marks.

CANAL TOWPATHS AND RIVERBANKS

In theory, towpaths are private property. Sometimes they are gated and locked, and you need a permit costing 25p. In practice you can usually walk along them without trouble. Riverbank paths may be closed off due to the problem of 'riparian' land, but often a right-of-way exists.

TRESPASS

If you go onto someone's land without permission, or stray off a right-of-way, you are trespassing. However, unless you do some damage, the landowner would get only token damages if he took you to court. A *'Trespassers will be Prosecuted'* notice has no real effect in practice, unless you do damage.

LONG DISTANCE FOOTPATHS

Although, as we have mentioned, many major trackways have existed since prehistoric times, they were then trade routes or military roads, and had often lost their purpose and disappeared by the late Middle Ages.

Some twenty years ago it was decided that in certain parts of the country, by using existing paths and purchasing or negotiating a right-of-way to link up the gaps, Long Distance Paths, offering walks of many miles, could be established.

With considerable effort a number of such routes have now been established, of varying lengths, and the number continues to grow. The Pennine Way, the South Downs Way, the Wolds Way, Offa's Dyke Path, the Ridgeway and many more, are now attracting thousands of walkers into the countryside and providing a real challenge to the experienced rambler.

WHEN TO WALK

Contrary to popular belief, high summer is not the best time for walking, It is frequently too hot, certain paths are closed by standing crops and heavy undergrowth can block narrow pathways.

In springtime other paths may be blocked voluntarily to save disturbing nesting birds, or spring sowing, while in winter the footpaths can be poached out by rain and become churned into swamps. So when do you go? Today, is the short answer. *Where* do you go is the real question. In the cold weather, go to the woods and valley bottoms. In summer to the shady tracks and windy moors. In autumn, enjoy the blazing colours of the woods and quietness on popular tracks, after the crowds have gone.

Whenever and wherever you go — enjoy yourself, and follow the Country Code.

Fig. 1

KARRIMOR
PAPOOSE
CHILD CARRIER

CHILDREN

By all means take the children. They can certainly cope with walks of five miles or more from about the age of six years. Don't try and do too much to start with, for very often children attempt more than they can manage.

Footwear is a problem, as they grow so fast. Stout shoes, or well fitting "wellies" with two pairs of socks, are usually sufficient, until they are older.

Take some food and warm clothing, and be very wary of allowing small children to carry a rucksack unless it is virtually empty. They get tired, and carrying your rucksack, theirs *and* the child can be very tiring.

Start with short 3-5 mile walks until you are sure they can manage more, but do **NOT** take children hill walking until they are old enough, equipped with proper clothing, including the right shoes or boots, and only when the weather is fine.

TAKING THE KIDS

Now for a little more detail. Many people are doubtful about taking children walking, yet those who do are amazed at how little trouble it is providing the trip is well planned.

Remember: Never take young children on a long walk if you are new to it yourself. You should be completely familiar with the planning and routine involved. If your children are really town-based, attempt a few *short* day-walks first and gradually introduce them into what they may expect.

It is often easier to take a baby under eighteen months than to take a toddler who is running everywhere and into everything at once, and tiring himself very quickly. Make stay-at-home arrangements for teenagers if they decide they would rather not accompany you. Remember that walking may be your idea of fun, not theirs, and it is unfair to drag them along against their will.

Children's interests in walking may be different from yours, and you will have to be ready to adapt if everyone is to really enjoy it. Keep the distance to be covered short so that you will have time to examine things along the way and answer the unnumerable questions which enter young minds as they go along. Be prepared, and allow extra time for rests—not necessarily because they will be tired but because they will become disinterested without a change in pace and procedure. Try to plan a walk which is interesting from the point of view of things to see i.e. old ruins, woodlands, deer parks, etc.

ROUTINE

If your day-trip is going to involve a change in a child's routine — in food, sleeping, and rules—try introducing the changed routine at home first. If necessary, take Teddy, or a favourite cuddly toy along too!

SAFETY

Safety can be a problem when toddlers are on a walking trip. They can easily wander off, injure themselves, or eat something poisonous. To alleviate the risk a very young child can be kept on a harness-rein, which is fine for short walks and it prevents the necessity of having adults constantly shouting commands at them. They can still explore within defined areas, and it is safe.

Where older children are concerned, they should be taught beforehand to follow out certain routines in given circumstances, and this can be practised locally in the park or local open space. If a child becomes detached from the rest of the party, he/she should:

1. Sit down on the spot and blow a whistle, which is always kept tied to his clothing. They will soon get bored with blowing it at home, and only use it when worried.
2. Stay on the spot until someone comes back for him.

You must try an explain the reasons for safety without instilling unnecessary fear in his mind. If you take children with you on a walk, remember that you are responsible for them and you should never take your eyes off them anyway.

EQUIPMENT FOR THE YOUNG

You can't buy a boot that will last a lifetime for a growing foot—but boots for children are still important. At the present time there are a number of children's boot styles which are popular for casual wear and can be bought in most shoe stores. However, buy something which is practical and don't be persuaded by your son/daughter into buying something which is purely and simply a high-fashion article. Remember their safety comes first. A well-fitting shoe or boot with a leather upper and a good cleated sole will be adequate for most walks, and a good quality 'wellington' boot with a heavy-duty cleated sole will be needed for muddy winter romps.

For a very young child or baby you will need a child carrier. Don't buy this without first trying it on *with the child in it.* The lower the weight, the heavier the load; the future walker should ride high on your back. You will need padded straps, plus pockets or a pounch for nappies and a bottle. Some carriers are both forward and backward facing, and you can choose one which you and your baby prefers. Remember that because he can wriggle around a fourteen-pound baby will feel heavier than a twenty-five pound pack! Try and swap over with your partner carrying the baby occasionally as you walk.

Older children can carry their own small daypack, and gives then an added sense of responsibility — they feel an important part of the gang.

Children's clothing etc., will be the same as yours, but in smaller sizes. Be certain that they take a warm hat and mittens, even in summer when it can turn decidedly chilly. A baby in a carrier will not be moving around like those actually walking and needs to be warmly wrapped up. In summer a hat suitable for keeping the sun off his head and face is essential. Disposable nappies will keep him comfortable and these can be packed in plastic bags.

Remember that if the kiddies are happy you will be happy too.

Chapter 2

CLOTHING AND FOOTWEAR

Walking is a healthy activity, and can be warm work. You therefore need to be continually adjusting your pace and garments to keep a warm yet even body temperature, and this is based on the *'layer'* principle.

The 'layer' principle for clothing applies as much to walking and rambling as it does to other outdoor activities. This principle states that two thin sweaters or shirts are warmer than one thick one, and that the maintenance of an even body temperature is of paramount importance. There is no need to delve into science, but it is a fact that extra insulation is obtained by 'layer' clothing because air is trapped between the garments and acts as a barrier to the outer air.

It must also be appreciated that since walking is warm work, much insulation will be lost if you start to perspire. With the layer principle, garments can be stripped off or zipped open at will, thus allowing the body to breathe and body moisture to escape.

Excellent synthetic materials, like Dacron and Hollofil etc., are now widely used for our-door kit and garments. Cotton and wool are the ideal materials for your outdoor clothing, with nylon and terylene synthetics much used for 'shell' protection against wind and weather.

STOCKINGS AND SOCKS

Socks are short, and stockings are long. Both pad the foot inside the boot. With modern socks, one pair is sufficient but two pairs are usually required, one short thick pair and one long knee-length thinner pair, plus a spare pair for a change, or if you get wet. The long pair can be pulled up over the trousers, while the short pair can be turned over the tops of the boots. Some people prefer two thick pairs, or a thick wool pair and a loop-stitched pair. Soft loop-stitched socks are the best for walking. Whatever the combination chosen, you must ensure that your socks are soft, well-washed and well fitting. They must not be too large or they will wrinkle, or too small, which will lead to cramped toes and discomfort—both will lead to blisters. I never wear new socks directly after purchase, but wait until they have been washed several times before going out in them. This ensures that any shrinking can be spotted and the fibres have had

14

time to soften. It is best to check that the socks are guaranteed against shrinkage before purchase, and then wash them according to instructions. I wear new socks around the house, and by wearing and washing, break them in just like new boots. Never wear darned socks, for be the darn never so neat, it will lead to blisters. Turn the socks inside out and trim off any loose strands, uneven stitching, or lumps.

Nylon socks have improved a lot in recent years and are *sometimes* preferred as under-socks, since they are usually seamless and can be easily washed and quickly dried, but I would never wear them for serious walking.

The important thing about your socks or stockings is that they should help to prevent blisters, rather than cause them. Put them on carefully, smoothing them onto the feet, and being sure they feel snug and comfortable.

FOOTWEAR

This section was going to be called 'Boots'. You *can* walk in shoes, but most serious walkers wear boots and prefer them whatever the season or weather. This said, it must be admitted that some great walkers, like John Hillaby, prefer shoes, mostly because they are lighter. Avoid heavy boots but do go for good quality, leather and workmanship.

Here again, avoid synthetics, which means you must buy leather footwear, and leather means money. However, your boots and socks will protect your feet from a great deal of hardship, so whatever else you may have to stint on, spend all you can afford on your boots. As with most things you'll get what you pay for, and anything costing (currently) less than £20 is unlikely to last long.

A good walking boot should:—

1. Be of leather, and not too heavy.
2. The uppers should be cut from one piece of leather, without seams on the side.
3. Have a sewn-in tongue. Many Continental boots do not have this feature.
4. Have a cleated, moulded or 'Vibram' sole. (Three common names for the same thing.) The sole should be *fairly* flexible, neither too rigid or too floppy.
5. The welt should be stitched. This is expensive but wears well, and the sole can be replaced when worn.
6. The laces should be secured by a system of steel hooks and rings and close the boot firmly and completely. Eyelet holes let in water.

7. They should be COMFORTABLE, the sole flexible and the inner well-padded.

Fig. 2

WALKING BOOT

VIBRAM SOLE

BUYING BOOTS

Buy your boots from an 'outdoor' stockist, one with a large selection and an experienced staff of walkers or hill-trekkers, who will advise you. Wear or borrow the required socks and aim to spend some time over selection.

Trying on the boots for a few moments in the shop is, at best, inadequate, for the longer you can take over your choice the better. In the better shops you will often find the staff prepared to let you take the boots and wear them at home for a few days. Providing you keep the bill and wear them only indoors, they will let you change them if they prove uncomfortable.

When trying them on, remember that the correct *length* is vital for boots will ease sideways in use, but cannot grow longer.

Your toes should not touch the end at all, but be free to wriggle slightly. Remember that the weight of a rucksack, or coming down a slope will thrust your feet forward and there must be space for them. If you thrust your feet well into the boots, you should be able to get your forefinger down inside the heel. Examine the boot carefully, and decide if it looks like a workmanlike well-finished article.

Ideally, your heel must not move, or by riding up and down inside the boot, you heels will blister. This means that the sole must flex and the boot bend with the foot.

I write this with feeling, for I am at present breaking in a new pair of boots and nursing some remarkable blisters. However, once the newness passes, the boots will (I hope) flex with my feet and the heels will fit snugly.

Try on as many pairs as you need to, until you are happy. Boots are too expensive to purchase quickly and the effects of badly fitting boots are too painful to contemplate lightly. Don't expect to pay much less than £20 for a decent pair of boots, and you can pay twice that, without any difficulty.

TROUSERS OR BREECHES

Don't wear jeans. They are tight, cold, useless as protection when wet, slow to dry, and split with disconcerting ease when straddling a fence or stile. It is, incidentally, always a good idea to have an extra row of stitches put on the seat-seam of your pants, as the strain there is considerable.

Jeans avoided, any old woollen or worsted trousers will do to begin with. Corduroy, needlecord, or tweed trousers are excellent, especially in the winter, and shorts are not to be disparaged in reliable summer weather. Be sure they are not too tight, and avoid chafe. This applies to underwear as well.

Once you get hooked on walking, it pays to invest in a pair of breeches. These can be worn with long socks in winter or with two pairs of short socks in summer, leaving the calves bare. Breeches come in various materials, thin for summer, thick for winter, but in all cases should have deep pockets fastened with buttons or velcro strips, a double seat, fastenings to open at the knee, and secure at the waist with a good wide belt.

GAITERS

Not everyone wears gaiters, but I believe everyone should, for they have many advantages. They prevent the trouser bottoms becoming saturated in long grass, help to keep water out of the boots when passing through dew, puddles or shallow streams, and collect a lot of mud that would otherwise spoil your clothing. They are usually made of nylon or canvas.

There are two types of gaiter, the short ankle-type or 'stop-tous' and the knee-length type, which hooks on to the bootlaces and fastens with a strap under the instep. Some have a zip at the back, while others have to be pulled on before you put on the boots. On balance, the zip-up type is better because the gaiters can be put on after you put on your boots and taken off at a lunch halt, to sit on or lay out the sandwiches on, or just because you feel them overheating your legs. Whichever type you choose though, make sure you wear them. I wear them all the time, except in very warm weather, and have never regretted it.

SHIRTS

Any old cotton shirt will do. Long sleeves are handy against sunburn or midges, for you can always roll a long sleeve up, but no way can you roll a short sleeve down. It should be long and comfortably loose, tucked in to avoid rucking. Many people wear T-shirts or roll-necked cotton sweaters, which in winter are very comfortable, but in summer it is often essential to have lots of buttons or a zip to undo, as both you and the day warm up.

NECKCLOTHES

A cravat, neckcloth or neckerchief, call it what you will, is often useful. I use an old teatowel, but if you can get hold of a long cotton towelling bar mat from your friendly neighbourhood pub, so much the better. It will keep the sun and wind from flaying your neck in summer, or a rough shirt from chafing. In autumn it keeps the rain from running down your neck, and in winter it keeps the wind out. Fashionable scarves in Indian silk are currently much worn, but they are not nearly so useful for drying the hands.

SWEATERS

Two thin ones are better than one thick one. I have a 'V'-necked lambswool one which I usually wear, and carry a roll-necked one which is only worn in the early morning when camping.

ANORAKS

It is hard to appreciate just how many varieties of anoraks are now available. Essentially, an anorak is a padded cross-stitched zipped jacket containing some insulating material. The best insulating material is down, but down jackets are expensive, often unsuitable in wet weather, and by the time you really need to buy one, you will have outgrown the contents of this book.

The snag with down (apart from the cost) is that while giving excellent insulation when dry, it is useless when wet, and it does (let's face it) tend to rain in Europe anywhere where it isn't very hot. You will therefore find that an anorak filled with some synthetic material, like Hollofil, or P2, will stay warm even when wet and will be considerably less expensive.

The term 'expensive' depends on how much you can afford, so concentrate on essential features. An anorak needs to:
1. Be hip length.
2. Have a collar (and if possible a hood).
3. Fasten with a strong zip.
4. Have a zip and pockets which are flapped.
5. Have flaps which secure with pop-studs or velcro strips.
6. Have sleeves which cover the wrists with integral elastic cuffs.

Fig. 3

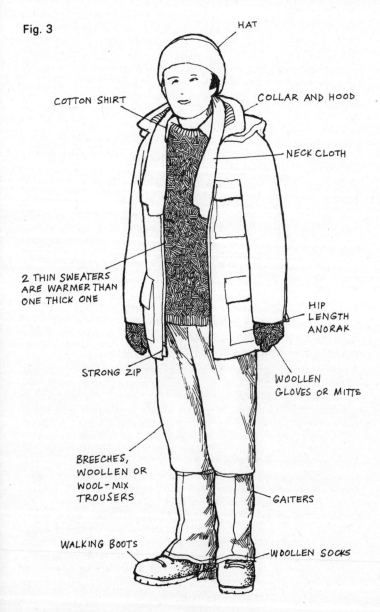

HAT

COTTON SHIRT

COLLAR AND HOOD

NECK CLOTH

2 THIN SWEATERS
ARE WARMER THAN
ONE THICK ONE

HIP
LENGTH
ANORAK

STRONG ZIP

WOOLLEN
GLOVES OR MITTS

BREECHES,
WOOLLEN OR
WOOL-MIX
TROUSERS

GAITERS

WALKING BOOTS

WOOLLEN SOCKS

Examine the material and manufacture carefully. Are the seams double stitched? Does it look like a well-made workmanlike job? You will never get more than you pay for, but it does pay to check that you are not getting less. You can, of course, get along without an anorak, wearing just a sweater and perhaps a fibre-pile, or sports jacket, but for the serious walker, anoraks are best, although Fibrepile jackets are currently very popular.

GLOVES
Gloves and Dachstein mitts are very popular, but any wool gloves will do, worn inside a leather pair in wet weather.

HATS
The head is like a radiator. If you are too cold, put a hat on. If you are too hot, take it off. Estimates vary, but is is broadly agreed that some 30% of the body's heat loss is from the head. Wool caps tend to be itchy, but are very comfortable when pulled down over the ears in winter. Carry some soft, warm, head covering, like a Balaclava or a cap to shed rain water. When walking in normal weather you will hardly need one, but when it gets chilly or windy you wil be glad you have it. In summer, something to protect your head from the sun is also very necessary.

'SHELL' CLOTHING
'Shell' clothing consists of waterproof and windproof garments to go over your outer clothing, and these are usually made of a synthetic material. The complete outfit consists of a long smock (or cagoule) and over-trousers. Both these items have certain essential features, which any you may purchase should possess.

The cagoule should be 'heavyweight', which means that it must be of a robust and durable material giving good insulation. You can buy thin 'cags', but while they weigh little and keep the rain out, they rip easily, especially when snagged on thorns, give little protection from the wind, and are inadequate in the winter. Ultimate Equipment have some good 'cags'.

Your cagoule should have a hood. The hood needs drawstrings, or even better, a wire-stiffened face-piece. It must open all the way down, for better ventilation, and all pockets and zips should be covered with flaps and close with studs or velcro strips.

The over-trousers must have gussets and zips wide enough in the leg for you to put them on over your boots when the weather changes.

There is no denying that wearing 'shell' clothing presents problems. To keep the rain out the garments keep body-heat in. This leads to perspiration, which can be just as unpleasant. A material called GORE-TEX may be the answer. Gore-tex is so constituted that body moisture is able to evaporate through minute perforations in the material, which are too small to let the larger rain drops to penetrate. A range of 'Shell' clothing in Gore-tex is now available for Berghaus. The claims regarding Gore-tex will be better established after a year or two's testing, but the garments themselves are well made, and attractive, although expensive at around £50 for a top and trouser suit. Which brings us to costs.

COSTS

Good gear is never cheap, but many items may already be in your possession or something else can be substituted, while others can be acquired one at a time thus saving one large outlay. The prices below are the average for good outdoor clothing. You can get it cheaper at end of season sales and by shopping around carefully.

Long walking stockings (3 pairs) at £3.50 per pair
Short socks (2 pairs) loop-stitched £2.25 per pair
Gaiters (short) or £4.00
Gaiters (long) £7.00
Boots ....£20 (average price)
Anorak/Walking Jacket....................................£25
Breeches £15
'Shell' clothing (other than Gore-tex)...............£25
Gloves or Mitts...£3.00
Hat £3.00

We have left out shirts, sweaters, sunglasses, because there is no need to buy these specially for walking. Indeed this is the chance to wear old clothing which you might otherwise throw away.

As you can see, there is little change from £100 and you still need some equipment. However, you don't need to buy new clothing, and provided you have good boots and an anorak, any old clothes will do.

Frequently people buy cheap gear, and return quickly to replace it with better equipment, when they realise the benefit. It is best to use old clothes to begin with and buy good new equipment as you need it, rather than spending good money on a set of inadequate gear at the start.

Chapter 3

EQUIPMENT

It is only fair to state that ramblers can get along pretty well to begin with without any equipment, apart from the clothing mentioned in the previous chapter, and a map. Many footpaths are well signposted and sufficiently walked, making them easy to follow. However, certain items soon become necessary and add to the fun. Also, since you intend to go on to longer walks in remoter areas, get the essential items early on and become proficient in their use.

MAPS

Biography is about chaps
And Geography is about maps.

The most popular map for rambling is the 1:25,000 O.S. Map. The 1:25,000 scale is where approximately 2½ inches on the map is equal to one mile on the ground. Also available, and very popular with outdoor folk, is the 1:50,000 scale. In sleaves they currently cost £1.40, while the flat-sheet versions are 90p. The 1:50,000 scale is one which gives less definition but requires half as many maps to cover the same amount of ground. The O.S. Outdoor Leisure series at £1.50 to £1.95 are excellent, and give footpaths as well as camp and caravan sites.

FOOTPATHS ON MAPS

On the right-hand edge of the map is a collection of 'conventional signs'. These are the marks, colours, or symbols used on the map to illustrate features on the ground. The footpaths are shown on English and Welsh (but not Scottish) 1:50,000, maps, by red dots. The bridleways are shown by red dashes. The 1:50,000 Scottish maps do not show footpaths, but their 1:25,000 series shows them in green.

It should be pointed out that the existence of a path on the map does not indicate a right-of-way on the ground, for there may be local bylaws or other short term restrictions.

From the O.S. map it is possible to work out circular walks of your own and with a good grasp of map reading, which we shall cover later, you have the basic skills for simple rambles.

Fig. 4

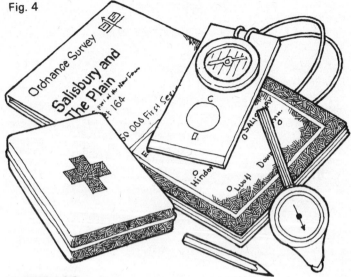

COMPASS

Most walkers use the Silva Compass, an accurate instrument which incorporates a compass and a protractor and is indispensible in all manner of ways to the walker. Silva Compasses are available in various models, at prices ranging from £3 upwards.

MAP MEASURES

Before you set out on your walk, you will want to know how far it is to your destination. You can, with experience, make a very accurate guess by calculating from the known scale and by using the squares of the National Grid which cover the map. On the 1: 50,000 each grid square side is one kilometre (⅝ mile), but a swifter and more accurate assessment can be made by using a map-measure.

This is a small instrument resembling a miniature barometer, with a distance dial. The dial can be set for various scales, and at the base is a milled travel-wheel.

Running the travel wheel over your chosen route on the map, will turn a distance dial and you can then read off the distance involved against the relevant map-scale. Map measures are very useful for rambling, for the footpaths rarely run in a straight line. Map measures cost about £3.65. See Fig. 4.

Once the distance is established, you can study the map for information on the degree of difficulty, or heights involved (see Naismiths Rule, Page 39), and make some estimate of how long your journey will take.

MAP CASES AND MAP CARE

A map case will protect your maps from rain, dirt, and if you are careful, the wind. I use a plastic envelope that used to hold a sweater. Try to avoid folding and unfolding the map more than necessary. Seams can be reinforced with masking tape (not cellotape or scotch-tape) and there are even special sprays which can strengthen the maps against hard use. Buy up to date maps.

FIRST AID KIT

A small first aid kit can be useful. You will certainly get blisters and the odd insect bite, sting, or grit in the eye, is always a possibility. The kit should contain:

1. A selection of plasters.
2. Some gauze or lint.
3. Some *Scholls* 'moleskin' for blisters.
4. A strip of Aspirin tablets.
5. Sun cream.
6. A small pair of scissors (for cutting plasters or bandage).
7. A mirror (for finding grit or flies in your eye).
8. *Optone* eyedrops.
9. A whistle: Six blasts is the mountain distress call.

You can expand this list considerably, but ounces count. You must cut down everywhere you can for that extra pound on your back will seem to weigh a lot more after a few miles! *Save ounces where you can.*

BINOCULARS

Yes, I know they are not essential, but they come in very handy, especially for picking out the route in bad weather, and you can get lightweight ones, with glass fibre shell cases.

A good pair, with a magnification of 8 x 30 or better, can greatly add to your enjoyment. For watching birds, scanning the countryside for routes, or simply for getting a better look at some far off landmark, a pair of binoculars will come in very handy.

RUCKSACK

Initially you can get along with the above items, and either have a sandwich in a pub or cafe at lunchtime, but it is easier to carry these and other items in a light frameless rucksack.

There is a whole range of rambler's rucksacks available at between £4-£15 and into this you can stuff your 'shell' gear, spare sweater and dry socks, sandwiches, first aid kit and, later on, a small stove and some food ready to make a hot meal.

Most outdoor shops will contain a selection of rucksacks, and if you are happy with day or half-day rambling then one of up to 20 litres capacity will be adequate. Get one with a couple of outside pockets so that your spare clothing can go in the main compartment, while the items you are going to need more frequently, like maps, chocolate, or whatever, can be kept readily available in one of the pockets. If you get a rucksack larger than you actually need, you will feel obliged to fill it, and carry extra weight. A very good day-sack is the Karrimor Bambiano 2, which has a front pocket, good comfortable shoulder straps, and costs only £6.50. The Tac-Pac also from Karrimor, is slightly larger, and suitable for hostelling.

Fig. 5

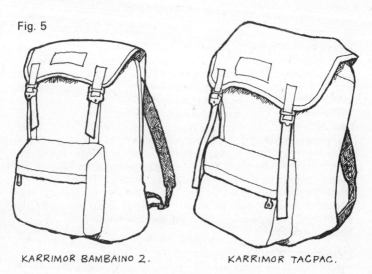

KARRIMOR BAMBAINO 2.   KARRIMOR TACPAC.

Chapter 4

MAP AND COMPASS

A good grasp of map and compass work is essential. Even in rural areas it is very easy to get lost or delayed, and in either case a knowledge of map and compass can save you a good deal of trouble.

Map and compass work really is perfectly simple providing you follow a few simple rules. Two of these are paramount and must be grasped at the start.

1. Keep the map 'set'.
2. Trust the compass.

Failure to obey these two basic rules causes most of the trouble, but there are other problems as well, so, assuming that you have at your elbow an O.S. map, scale 1:50,000; a Silva compass; a pencil and some paper, we can proceed.

THE MAP

The basic tool is the Ordnance Survey (O.S.) map, available from most outdoor shops and bookshops. Maps come in different scales. The two scales most suitable, as we said in Chapter 3, are the 1:50,000 and the 1:25,000, the latter being marginally better in the hills and remote country.

The first step is to open the map out flat, lay it on a table, stand back, and look at it. Notice the high ground, the tilt of the land, the main towns and rivers. Try to get some feeling for the *shape* of the land the map represents. Note also the 'magnetic variation' which is the difference between 'Magnetic North', where all compass needles point, and the other 'Norths', *True North* (the North Pole) and *Grid North* (the top of the map). Note also the annual change in this 'variation', (between Magnetic and Grid North) and the date of the map. All this information will come in handy later.

CONVENTIONAL SIGNS

Down the right-hand edges of the map are the illustrated conventional signs. These are marks, letters and colours representing features on the ground. It's a good family game to get round the table and practise naming and finding conventional signs on the map, and an excellent method of learning to identify them. Don't just stick to 'wind pumps' and 'youth hostels'. Find 'trig' points and 'concave' slopes, and heathland, road junctions and trackways.

SCALE AND DISTANCE

You must get some idea of distance. On the 1:50,000 map, each side of the grid square measures 1 kilometre — and a kilometre is ⅝ mile. Get a feeling for the scaled-down distance on the map, and what it may mean scaled-up on the ground.

With a local map find the distance from your house to the local pub, your place of work, the kid's school. This is the distance off the map, that is, as the crow flies. As the little devil walks up and down hills it's probably further, and you can work that out by studying contour lines.

CONTOUR LINES

Do try and read the contours. On the O.S. 1:50,000 they are 50 feet apart, but the 'spot' or 'trig' heights are given to the nearest metre (3'3"). Contour lines join up *points of equal height*, and run at that level all over the terrain. One thing that often foxes people is to know from the contours whether a feature is a spur or a re-entrant. (Fig. 6). A spur projects out from the land mass, while a re-entrant is just the opposite, a valley running into it. In order to tell the difference, note firstly that the contour values (or heights) which are given at intervals along the line, are given to read *facing uphill*. This noted, you can compare one contour value with another, and note the increase or decrease. Finally, common sense, for rivers and streams do not normally run up spurs or along the tops of hills.

You can tell a lot from contours. For example, if the contours are even , the slope is even. If they are close together, the slope is steep. If far apart, the slope is gentle. If they are far apart at the top and spread out at the bottom, they are convex slopes. If they are close at the top, then widen out, it's concave. In open or wild country you will need to use the contours, so start learning about them from the start. The map may be flat but the ground isn't. The contours indicate just how much climbing up and down your walk will involve, and even tell you if your route will 'go' at all. It's really quite easy if you practise hard.

'SETTING' or ORIENTING THE MAP

People go off in the wrong direction because they hold the map like a book, and not in line with the features on the ground. To 'set' or 'orient' the map, you quite simply hold it so that *the features on the map are always in line with the features on the ground*. (Fig. 7).

This may well mean holding the map upside down. So what? You can still read it like that, and it stops you turning left instead

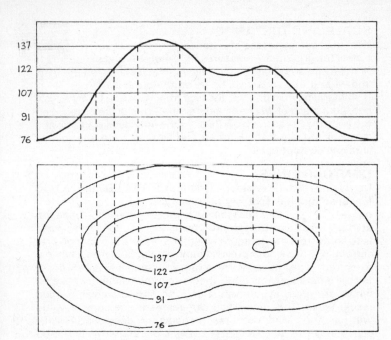

CONTOURS OF A HILL WITH A COL

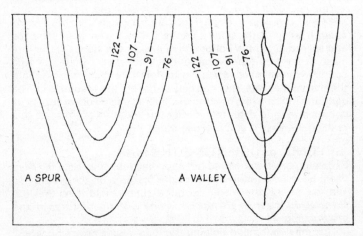

DIFFERENCE BETWEEN A SPUR AND A VALLEY OR RE-ENTRANT

Fig. 6   Contour lines

Fig. 7

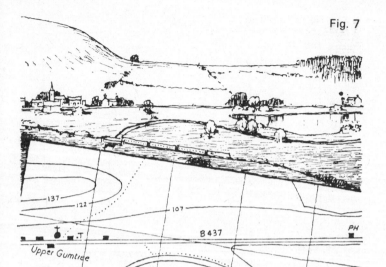

—137—122— ——107——

B 437 PH

Upper Gumtree

R. Na

"Setting" the map

of right, or searching for features on one side, which are in fact on the other. So, *set* the map, and keep it *'set'*. Always!

MAP REFERENCES (M.Rs.)

People are always giving and receiving incorrect map references. It's a very common error. Have a look at the map again. It is criss-crossed with the blue lines of the National Grid, and you will notice that each line is numbered.

Taking our example (Fig. 8) M.R. 9041 gives you the intersection of two grid lines, an 'easting' 90, and a 'northing' 41. They intersect at the *bottom left-hand corner* of a grid square. That square No. is 9041.

'Eastings' are the lines which run vertically up the map, and advance across it from west to east—90, 91, 92 etc., hence 'Eastings', 'Northings' run horizontally across the map, and run in series from south to north, hence 'Northings'. When giving a reference, remember that 'Eastings' always come before 'Northings'. To fix our map reference within the square 9041 we divide the sides of the grid square into tenths, either mentally, or

29

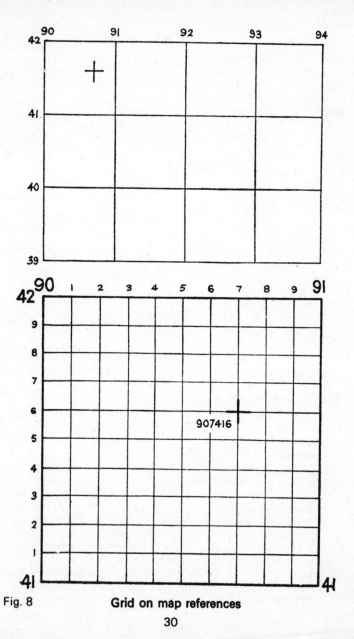

Fig. 8   **Grid on map references**

with a little divided ruler called a 'roamer', and go $^7/_{10}$ along the 'easting' direction (907) and $^6/_{10}$ up the 'northing' direction (416) and we get a M.R. 907416. A good way of remembering the correct routine is to murmur to yourself that you always go 'Along the corridor, and up the stairs'.

COMPASS WORK

You can get along for a while without a compass, but you will soon want one. Buy a Silva — a very popular make — and examine it closely. Note the names of the parts (Fig. 9), as otherwise the following explanations will be obscure.

'SETTING THE MAP WITH THE COMPASS

If you can't find out where you are from features on the ground, this is a useful skill. You need to find North and the routine is as follows:—

1. First set the *magnetic variation* on the compass.

   This is quite important for even a small variation can lead to confusion. If the variation is 8°, that will be a minute difference on the compass, but the 8° angle will 'subtend' or widen as it moves away from you, and if you are trying (say) to identify one of two hills a few miles away, forgetting that variation can have you marching merrily on the wrong one.

2. Then turn the compass housing until the orienteering arrow lies under the compass needle.

3. Place the compass on the map, and turn the MAP until the grid lines on the map lie parallel with the orienteering lines on the compass. This gives you magnetic north, and you now know which way you are facing, your map is 'set', and features on the ground should start to fall into place on the map. Even if you want to march South, you know which way to turn.

ANNUAL CHANGE

The magnetic variation changes annually. You may note on your map that the variation is 8.25°W in 1974 and decreasing ½° in eight years. In 1978 therefore the variation will be 8°.

The date of the map is also your clue to nasty surprises which, according to the map, should not be there — like a housing estate on virgin land, a sudden planatation of trees, or a motorway. Look at the date of the map and reflect that a lot can happen in a few years.

FINDING YOUR POSITION BY COMPASS BEARINGS (RESECTION)

For resection (Fig. 10), you need two or more identifiable

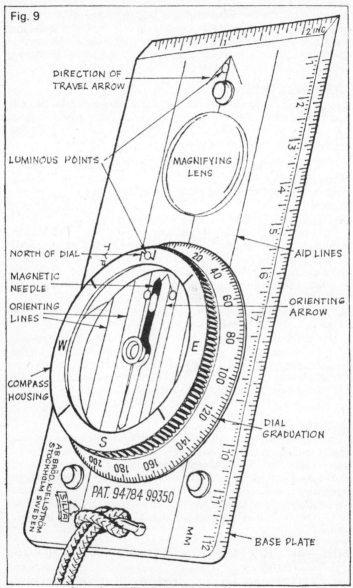

Fig. 9

DIRECTION OF TRAVEL ARROW

MAGNIFYING LENS

LUMINOUS POINTS

AID LINES

NORTH OF DIAL

MAGNETIC NEEDLE

ORIENTING LINES

ORIENTING ARROW

W

E

COMPASS HOUSING

S

DIAL GRADUATION

AB BRÖD. KJELLSTRÖM STOCKHOLM SWEDEN

SILVA

PAT. 94784 99350

MM

BASE PLATE

The Silva compass

32

landmarks on the ground that you can also find on the map. A far-off peak or river bend will do, but try and get them at a good angle to each other. Take the compass and point the travel arrow directly at the landmark. Then, holding it steady, swivel the housing until the needle and orienting arrow match, north to north. Now read off the bearing at the index number point, and note it down. Repeat this process with the other landmarks, until you have two or more magnetic bearings to the landmarks. These have to be converted into grid bearings before you can draw them on the map. This is where the magnetic variation comes in. To convert magnetic bearings into grid bearings, you *SUBTRACT* the magnetic variation. For example:—

> Magnetic, or compass bearing = 280°
> Magnetic variation of 8°   = –8°
> Map or 'grid' bearing   = 272°

To apply this, set the first (magnetic) bearing on the compass, and then turn the dial to deduct the variation. This automatically gives you the grid bearing. Forget the magnetic bearing, you no longer need it. Place the direction line, or the edge of the compass, over the first landmark, with the landmark as close to the compass dial as possible. Then, keeping the line over the landmark, swivel the compass until the orienteering lines are parallel to the grid lines, with the orienteering arrow pointing north.

Then, at the point where the sighting line runs off the compass, make a dot on the map with a pencil, to make a mark. (You only need this if the distance to the landmark is considerable, and too far for the compass edge).

Now, using the compass edge as a ruler, run a pencil line from the landmark back through the map mark, well back towards your position, which is somewhere along that line. Repeat the process with the second and subsequent landmarks, and your position is where they cut the first line.

In doing this, we have turned *magnetic bearings* into *grid* or *map bearings*. To get a compass bearing to march on, you must be able to reverse this process.

GRID BEARINGS INTO COMPASS BEARINGS

First, identify your position and objective, and then lay the compass edge down as a line connecting the two points. Now turn the compass housing until the orienting lines are parallel to the grid lines. Ignore the compass needle at this point.

Now, read off the grid bearing at the index point. This is a GRID bearing, and you need a *magnetic* or compass bearing. To convert the bearing you *ADD* the magnetic variation. To use our previous example:—

Grid Bearing	=	272°
Magnetic variation	=	+8°
Magnetic Bearing	=	280°

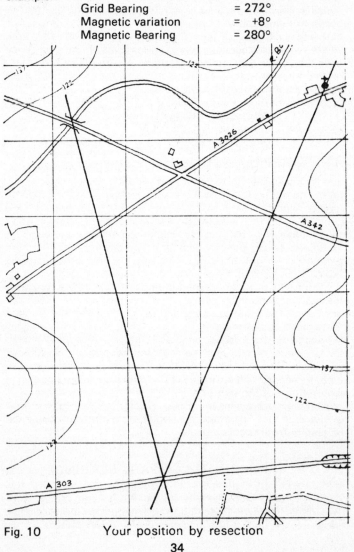

Fig. 10   Your position by resection

Putting the map away, set the compass dial to 280° and swivel yourself around until the north point of the magnetic needle lies over the north point of the orienting arrow. Keep these needles overlapping, and march off in the direction indicated by the travel arrow, which will be 280°, and the direction of your destination.

So, remember this is what you do with the variation:—

Compass (Mag.) to Map (Grid) you SUBTRACT it.

Map (Grid) to Compass (Mag.) you ADD it.

It is simpler just to remember one of these, and an easy memonic is 'MUGS' — Magnetic Unto Grid Subtract. Just recite this to yourself, reversing the process if applicable (GUMA) and you won't go far wrong.

'EAST' AND 'WEST' VARIATIONS OR DECLINATIONS

In some parts of the world, North America for example, they have an easterly variation or declination, as well as a westerly one. It depends on the relative position of the Magnetic Pole. With an Easterly variation you reverse the process for the Westerly one that is:

Compass to Map—add the Easterly variation

Map to Compass—subtract the Easterly variation

BACK BEARINGS

Perhaps the land is featureless in front, but there is a handy television mast behind, so to get a *back bearing* on it is simple, and you can march away from it, checking behind you periodically. To establish a back bearing is simple. If the bearing you are marching *on* is over 180°, to get a back bearing you *subtract* 180°. If it is *less* than 180° you add 180°. Simple isn't it! See this example:—

Bearing 045° (less than 180°) + 180° = Back Bearing 225°.

Bearing 260° (more than 180°) – 180° = Back Bearing 080°.

Back bearings are useful. Say you march on 250° for an hour in fog, and don't arrive where you should. You decide to retrace your steps. Deduct 180°, bearing 070°, and march back on that for one hour. You can't be so far from base, so start blowing that whistle, and help is at hand!

There is a great deal more to map and compass work, and a lot of it is experience and instinct. Our book 'MAP AND COMPASS' also published in this series, will tell you all you need to know about this useful and fascinating skill, and you will, after a while, learn to use the tilt of the land, the direction of a stream, the shadows of the sun, and the breeze on your cheek, as well as map and compass, as aids to travelling fast and arriving safely in the remote places. This is fell-craft and it comes with time, but a good grasp of map and compass work is an essential outdoor skill, even for beginners. You don't need a mountain. The local pub, your first few rambles, or the dining room table will do quite well to start with.

Chapter 5

MAKING A START

Don't start by attempting to walk the Pennine Way. Start slowly and over short distances. You have to break in your boots, harden your feet, toughen your muscles, get your gear organized and comfortable, and gain some experience. Let us start by considering a few day, or half-day trips.

BREAKING IN THE BOOTS
Wear them around the house in the evening and before going to bed put on more polish or Mars-oil and allow it to soak in overnight. Polish them again the next night when the polish has soaked well in. Then wear them for short walks down to the shop or pub. John Merrill reckons it takes 500 miles to break in a pair of boots! Light, flexible boots will be broken in after about 50 miles, while the stiffer the boot, the longer it takes. For a stiffer boot, you must expect to walk about a hundred miles before you feel at home in them.

Meanwhile, as a start in map-reading, also work out a few short routes of up to three miles for your first walk, off your local map. You will find plenty of open space on the local heath, along a river bank or towpath, and learn a lot about your local area as well as about map reading. These should suffice to settle in the gear and reveal a few aches and pains.

HARDENING THE FEET
Your feet are your friends, so look after them. Nothing is more depressing than a pair of aching 'dogs'. Keep them clean, frequently washed and dusted with talc. Clip the nails short, and go to a chiropodist for treatment for any corns or bunions. It has been found useful to rub the feet with methylated or surgical spirits. This is said to harden the feet and prevent blisters. It is worth trying, but I remain unconvinced, and rest my faith on comfortable footwear and well-washed socks for if you harden your feet with spirit, blisters can form *under* the hard skin.

TIME AND DISTANCE
The general concensus says that 2½ miles (4 km) per hour is a good average pace across country, taking the rough with the smooth, and assuming that no steep hills are involved and that the route does not degenerate into a scramble.

In wilder country, a better method is to use Naismith's Rule, which allows for ups and downs and will help you to read contours.

NAISMITH'S RULE

"Estimate an hour for every three miles off the map plus one hour for every 2,000 ft. (650m)." This is for the *unladen walker.* If you are carrying a loaded rucksack, you must increase the time allowance.

As you will have learned from the contours section in the previous chapter, you can easily calculate the amount of climbing up and down along your route, and a little experience will soon enable you to estimate the time of your journey quite accurately.

DISTANCES

How far should you travel? Initially, until your feet and boots are working happily together, short circular walks of about five miles in an afternoon will be adequate. Then build up to ten miles, with a decent lunchtime halt, and even for the experienced rambler, 12-15 miles will probably be sufficient for a day out, especially in the winter half of the year, when the days get short. A great deal depends on the time of the year. Long summer days give you a lot more time to reach your destination than the short foggy variety. Always aim to do less than you could do. It is better to have energy in hand at the end of the day, rather than arrive home exhausted. It's supposed to be fun, remember!

HOW TO WALK

There is more to this than just putting one foot in front of the other. Walking is an art, and like all arts it needs skill and practice.

SPEED

The basic rule is to adopt a steady even pace which you can maintain all day across all sorts of terrain, without getting overheated, and without excessive fatigue.

Swinging the arms may help to carry you along and if this gets your hands cold or puffy on a winter's day, you can always wear gloves or mitts. Try and follow the centre of the track, without wandering from side to side, but don't be afraid to go down, or lose hard won height, if an easier or safer route presents itself below. This is better than forcing your way along unsuitable ground.

UPHILL AND DOWN

Going uphill, take short regular steps, like a staircase, rather than massive lunges from one foothold to another. Coming down, keep the weight forward and don't rest back on your heels, for a jarring downhill descent like this can be more tiring than an uphill climb. Be cáreful coming down on wet rock, grass or mud, for your feet can slip from beneath you. If you find a pair, light heel-crampons are a useful buy and should be worn in slippery conditions. (Fig. 14 Page 55).

RIDGEWALKING
On the downs or hills, it is often better to choose the track below the crest. These are usually sheep runs, but they are often wide enough to walk on, and keep you out of the wind. In high winds, keep away from the edge of steep cliffs and escarpments. In pack and cagoule you offer considerable resistance to the wind and a sudden gust could blow you over. Walking into the wind can prove very tiring so shelter from its direct effects if you can.

ENERGY
If you are not used to walking, and try to do too much, you will rapidly get tired, but quite often this tiredness is due to lack of food. Your normal calorie intake is not usually sufficient for a hard day's exercise. Adequate energy means regular snacks rather than enormous breakfasts and lunches. This point is worth making even though most poeple eat too much in their normal daily life. They eat too much *and* take little exercise apd are therefore overweight and unfit. Regular walks plus the correct food, taken at the correct times, will give you the necessary fitness and energy and you will probably lose excess weight as well.

A good breakfast before you start, and regular snacks throughout the day will give you sufficient energy to carry on, and if you feel yourself getting tired, stop, eat some chocolate, and put the feet up before you continue. You need food with high calorific content; nuts, raisins, chocolate, glucose — not stodge.

HALTS
Unless your walk has a specific objective where you intend to halt anyway, aim for regular, but infrequent stops.

The old marching British Army halted for ten minutes in every hour for a drink and a rest, and no other halts were permitted. They covered four miles an hour like that, carrying up to 48 lbs. of kit. You should not carry more than 20 lbs.

If you keep stopping you will never get anywhere, and so fritter away the day, but if you are happy like that, then why not? However, try and keep going. In your initial planning, take note of possible places for a mid-morning cup of coffee, the lunch break, and the evening stop.

PUBS AND CAFES

If your lunchtime halt is at a pub, good manners and a little tact will not go amiss. This may seem an impertinent point, but unfortunately some ramblers have managed to put the backs up of many publicans and tradesmen, and therefore extra care is needed to restore good relations. Wipe the mud off your boots — or make an obvious and valiant attempt to do so or take them off. If you eat your sandwiches inside, buy something to go with them and try not to antagonise the locals. Ramblers have been barred from pubs and cafes in some areas after one group or another has hogged the fire, spread mud or pools of water in the bar, or generally treated someone else's business as their exclusive (and free) facility. Think of the other people, including other ramblers, who share these public places with you, and show a little consideration. It will pay off for us all in the end.

RUBBISH

Take your rubbish home, or place it in a proper litter bin which is there for that purpose. If you have the patience pick up other people's rubbish as well. Rubbish begets rubbish and everyone must do all they can to *KEEP BRITAIN TIDY*.

GETTING OUT AND BACK

If you *drive* to your starting point, leave the car in a car park or somewhere out of the way where it won't cause an obstruction. Farmers work a seven-day week, and if the cows can't get to the milking shed because your car is across the gateway — hard luck car! Make sure that the lights and radio are off, and that you will not sink axle deep in mud. Leave some newspapers and comfortable shoes, and perhaps even a change of clothing, in the car boot. You don't want wet clothes and muddy boots inside the car.

If you are going by bus or train, check the small print in the timetables carefully, especially at weekends and in the winter, for in country districts the bus services are, to say the least, spasmodic, while weekend train times often differ from the weekday ones.

WINTER WALKING

Remember that in winter, which can be the best season for walking, you will not have a lot of daylight. It can get dark by 4 p.m., or even earlier if the weather is bad. Have some reflective strips on your rucksack and walk *facing the traffic* in country lanes. It is also a very good idea to wear something light and you should carry a flashlight and make sure the cars can see you clearly, or be sure you can see them.

If you are going anywhere remote you should also have:

1. A tent.
2. A sleeping bag.
3. A survival bag.
4. Spare clothing.
5. Spare food.
6. A companion.

Don't start off by heading into the hills in mid-winter. By the time you are ready to do so you should have acquired all these items, plus the necessary experience. If you are going out in in the hills in snow, you also need:

1. Crampons.
2. An ice axe.

However, having got this far we now teeter on the edge of scrambling or hilltrekking — and that's another story. So let us carry on with simple lowland rambling, and off we go!

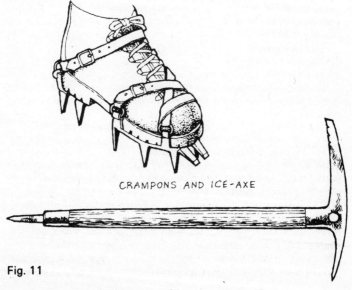

CRAMPONS AND ICE-AXE

Fig. 11

Chapter 6

PROGRESSIVE RAMBLING

A ramble is less than an expedition yet more than a walk. It needs planning.

By this stage of the book, you should have assembled your kit, hardened your feet, brushed up on map and compass and, most important, decided if you like walking or not. If you have, and it tends to be an all or nothing thing, then you have three fairly progressive options open to you, and you can take them all in due course. They are:

1. Day rambling.
2. Weekend walking.
3. Long distance footpaths.

If we look at these in that order, we can also discover what extra kit and skills you will need as your trips get longer. A series of progressive walks will soon provide the experience, and you can acquire any extra items of kit, as you need them.

DAY WALKING
A day walk can cover a distance of up to 20 miles, and perhaps a little more for the fit and experienced walker. The first three considerations, and they will affect all your decisions over all these walks, are:—

1. The season.
2. The weather.
3. The terrain.

Compare a summer Sunday walk along the Thames Valley, with a winter walk across the Pennines and you'll see what we mean.

PLANNING YOUR DAY WALK
After some half-day rambles, a full day walk should be within your grasp, and it just means an extension of existing skills and planning longer routes, with more food, and tighter timing.

If you aim to go on a long day walk next weekend, then on Wednesday you should start (1) by studying the weather forecasts and (2) getting the maps or guides out. Work out your routes and times, and, from the map, prepare a route card with start and finish, tracks to follow and timings. Most footpath guides give adequate guidance on these points anyway.

ROUTE CARDS

A route card is simply a collection of bearings, distances and estimated timings for your proposed walk.

Once prepared, it should then be checked, and if you are *going anywhere at all remote,* leave a copy with some responsible person who will at least have some idea where you are if you don't come back on time. This may be quite superflous for the aforementioned summer walking pub-crawl along the Thames, but it's still a good habit to get into. Apart from the safety element, a route card will also concentrate the mind most wonderfully — can you *really* do 18 miles over that country? If not, you'll miss the train — get the idea?

Also, if you are going to be out all day and walk that distance, you will need to take a full scale of kit, and if a hot mid-day meal is required, you'll need a stove if no cafe or pub presents itself. You *can* manage on a vacuum flask of tea and a packet of sandwiches but a fresh brew is a great comfort, and cooking can be fun.

STOVES AND FUELS

There is quite a wide range of stoves available, and five types of fuel. The fuel governs the stove, for each fuel has advantages and disadvantages, as you will see. The fuels are:

1. Solid fuel.
2. Gas.
3. Paraffin.
4. Petrol.
5. Meths.

Solid fuel is quite good for the rambler, but cooking times are a little slow. In gas stoves the 'Gas' used is butane, which will not gasify at temperatures below 1°C, so it is pretty useless in winter, but very good at other times. Paraffin and petrol stoves are fine providing you are very careful when lighting and filling them and don't mind carrying spare fuel, but for a day trip the stove itself will usually contain more than enough for your hot lunch and brews.

Most stove manufacturers have a wide range of stoves, and thanks to the lightweight camping and backpacking market, they all have a lightweight version, suitable for the rambler. Any good outdoor stockist can show you the range and give you good advice. Three stoves worth mentioning are the *Trangia* — which burns meths, the *SVEA 123* — a petrol stove, and the *Optimus 99.* The *Camping Gaz Globetrotter,* with its protective cookset is

43

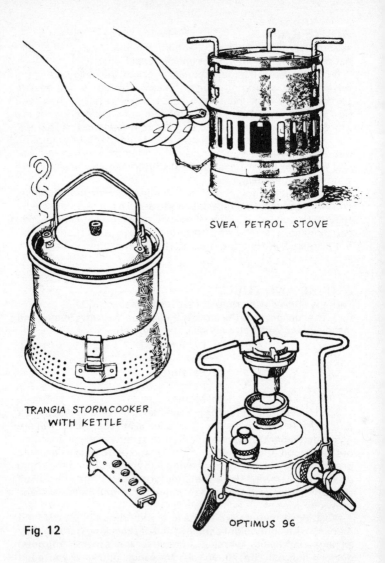

SVEA PETROL STOVE

TRANGIA STORMCOOKER
WITH KETTLE

OPTIMUS 96

Fig. 12

also much used, especially by summer walkers, and at less than
£10, is a reasonable purchase.

Together with a stove, you will need an aluminium cookset, a plastic spatula or ladle, and of course a set of K.F.S. eating irons and a mug. Wherever possible, choose aluminium or plastic for plates, mugs etc. Ounces make pounds, and pounds make kilos, so save ounces where you can.

COSTS

Lightweight petrol stove (average price) £15
Cookset £2
K.F.S. £1
Mug 20p

FOOD

The easiest way to calculate your food requirements is to prepare a food chart. The illustration (Fig. 13), covers a weekend walk, and will give you the idea. Simply list the meals and what you would like to eat (or are able to cook) and then by adding it up you arrive with a shopping list, and a good idea of weight.

	DAY 1	DAY 2	DAY 3	SUNDRIES	TOTAL SHOPPING LIST
Breakfast	4 eggs 4 sausages 2 slices bread 2 mugs tea	4 eggs 4 rashers bacon	4 eggs 4 rashers bacon	Butter (lb) Salt Tea bags (6) 1 large loaf	1 doz eggs 1 lb butter ½ lb sausages 1 large loaf Salt 8 rashers bacon (l lb)
Lunch	2 teas 2 apples 2 cheese sandwiches	2 teas 2 oranges Ham sandwiches	2 apples Corned beef sandwiches Tea	1 lb apples 2 lb oranges Tea bags (6)	1 lb apples 4 oranges 1 lb ham ½ lb corned beef
Dinner	Meat stew 2 teas	Steak and Kidney Pie Rice pudding Tea	Spaghetti Bolognese 2 oranges Tea	Tin opener Sugar Tea bags (6) 2 oranges	1 tin stew 1 tin steak and kidney 1 tin spaghetti bolognese 1 tin rice pudding
Supper	Biscuits 2 teas	Ham sandwiches Tea	Biscuits Tea	Biscuits Tea bags (6)	1 packet biscuits 24 tea bags Sugar Water (?)

Fig. 13

FLUIDS AND CONVENIENCE FOODS

You will also need to replace fluids lost during the day, with either hot drinks (tea or coffee, some glucose drink, or plain water). Unless it is available en route you will need to take one quart of water at least. A collapsible plastic bottle is ideal for transporting water. If you check the map and find that there are streams available for your water supply, remember that they may well be dry or polluted.

There is no longer any need to lug heavy tins of soup or stew into the country. Most outdoor shops have a wide range of prepacked convenience foods which, with a little water and a quick stir, soon become an appetising meal. Strip off as much packaging as possible, for most of it is just extra weight. You can also buy the ingredients and prepare your own convenience foods.

HOME COOKING

Apart from sandwiches, which can be wrapped in cling-film, foil or polythene bags, you can always cook a stew at home, put it in a sealed Tupperware container and re-heat it on your stove, in the field. Certain meals should not be re-heated, but in general, any pre-cooked dish which can be frozen can also be safely re-heated. However, make certain that you bring it to the boil and keep it bubbling gently for at least 10 minutes. Also make sure that you pack it so that it cannot spill over or leak into your other gear.

COOKING STORES

Most experienced walkers carry a little set of cooking stores and gadgets. These stay inside a plastic bag in one pocket of the rucksack and consist of such items as:—

1. Salt
2. Sugar
3. Cooking oil — in plastic bottle with good screw top.
4. Tin opener & corkscrew
5. Matches
6. Water purifying tablets.

Add to this list as you wish.

Don't take butter unless you also take one of the new compact insulated containers produced for campers. Personally I'm against butter for in summer it will melt and in winter you can't spread it. Take a light cooking oil for frying and some bread or crispbread with some cheese, which can also be pre-wrapped in cling-film or foil—but remember that cheese can become oily and runny in hot weather, so it needs to be well wrapped.

DAY WALKING ROUTINE

For a *day-walk* you will need to take apart from the usual clothing you wear:

1. Spare socks.
2. Shell clothing.
3. First aid kit/whistle.
4. Map(s). 1:25,000, or Outdoor leisure series.
5. Compass.
6. Route card.
7. Food (and stove for cooking).
8. Dry/warm clothing.
9. Money.
10. Timetable.

Have all this checked, packed in your rucksack, and ready the night before. Listen to the late radio or T.V. weather forecast.

Try and make an early start for half an hour lost in the morning can keep the pressure on all day.

On the walk try and stick to your plan if only to see just how realistic your home planning is but allow time to SEE the countryside. It's a ramble, not a race!

Once home again, clean up the gear, wash and polish off the boots, allowing them to dry gently away from direct heat. Wash plates and KFS, put dirty clothes on one side ready to wash, and be sure all your maintenance is done — including foot repairs, before you collapse in front of the fire. A good soak in a hot bath is very comforting to aching limbs, but maintenance comes first.

Many people say they hate 'routine'. I agree. However, certain things have to be done and a routine for doing them enables you to do them quickly and accurately and gives you more free time. All this will be vital when you go out for overnight rambles.

WEEKEND WALKING

A weekend walk is a lot more than a day trip times two. You will need camping and outdoor living skills as well as the ability to walk up to forty miles across country in two or three days. You *can* use hotels and hostels for the overnight stop, but they put the cost up considerably.

That said, a weekend trip is the next logical step after considerable day walking experience has been acquired.

LATERAL OR CIRCULAR?

Do you want to walk in a circle and return to your starting place, or are you walking in a line between two points? The former is easier to plan but harder to find. Getting to the starting point and home again is a problem with lateral walking, but you must start planning such walks for future use and present experience, so get out those maps and timetables.

Terrain is probably the governing factor, for the more urbanized areas do not readily produce forty miles of rambling on one lateral or circular route. Weekend walking usually means somewhere deep in the country.

WHERE TO GO

For a weekend walk, you can leave the local areas and look at wilder, but still mild outdoor areas (in summer anyway). The Chilterns and the Cotswolds, the South Downs, the Peak District and *parts* of the Lake District and Highlands are all suitable

47

areas. The Ridgeway and the South Downs Way could all be walked in two weekends, and overall, if you have the time, weekend walking is probably the most satsifactory pastime for the committed rambler. Try and go at least once a month, so that you stay fit enough.

ACCOMMODATION

If you decide to stay in hotels or hostels, you will usually find that the available accommodation, especially in the summer months is booked up well in advance. Don't expect to find an empty room the following weekend if you ring up on Monday. You need to plan a month ahead, and think of pubs, private houses and cafes, as well as hotels and hostels. In the winter many guest houses and summer 'lets' are closed — you can't win! (See next chapter.)

CAMPSITES

To camp *anywhere* you need permission. That's a fact. In the more remote parts, out of sight is usually out of mind, providing you behave yourself, don't start fires, and take your litter home. If you camp on anyone's land, and everywhere is somebody's land, you should get permission, and if you are caught without it you can be ordered off. To find an empty pitch in a campsite, you need to book, or risk disappointment at the fag-end of the day. A list of campsite guides is given in the last chapter. On the Continent there is much greater scope for free camping, but, as a general rule, you need permission.

WEEKEND WALKING EQUIPMENT

The biggest items — in terms of importance, size and expenditure for the weekend walker/camper are:—

1. Rucksack.
2. Sleeping bag.
3. Tent.
4. Safety gear (including spare boot laces)

If you hostel, or stay in hotels all the time you can dispense with (2) and (3), but wherever you sleep you will need a larger rucksack than the day rambler's little backpack. (See Hostelling, Chapter 9).

Karrimor, Berghaus and Camp Trails, are three major rucksack manufacturers of quality equipment. Bag sizes are now given in litres to indicate capacity and something around a 50 litre bag will be adequate. This compares with a day walking bag of up to only 20 litres capacity and an expedition bag of 60 plus. One too small is more of an embarrassment than one to big, but with a stuff-sack strapped underneath to hold the tent or sleeping bag and sleeping pad, a 50 litre bag should be big enough for even a week-long trip. A big bag tempts you to carry more than you need. Ounces make pounds, etc . . .

SLEEPING BAGS AND PADS
You will need a sheet-sleeping bag for hostelling, although they can be hired at the hostel. Even with a proper bag you will also need cotton liners or inners to keep the bag itself clean. Down-filled bags are now *very* expensive and especially in the damp U.K. climate, many people are turning to bags with a synthetic filling like Hollofil or P2. Down is not very suitable in a damp climate as it loses its insulating properties when wet.

'Point-Five', Blacks, Polywarm, and many other manufacturers have a wide range of bags at an even wider range of prices. Go to a good stockist and examine the selection. You will also need an airbed, or a ground pad unless you are used to sleeping on the cold hard ground.

TENTS
Tents can always be hired. Do not invest in a tent until you are sure you are going to need and use it regularly, and equally sure which type of tent you want. The range, in quality, price and destined use is quite literally incredible, and expanding yearly. A mistake can be expensive, for tents are not cheap.

Much of this expansion and development is change for change's sake, and the effect in practice is as much to baffle the customer as to satisfy a need. Lightweight tents suitable for the rambler are available at all sorts of prices, and when you decide to buy one, read up reports in the camping magazines, like 'Camping' or 'Practical Camper', go to a competent stockist and explain your needs. A rambler needs a lightweight tent weighing around 2.5 to 3.5 kilos. The lightness is often obtained by skimping strength, but the strength is often retained by using expensive materials and careful manufacture. It follows that a good lightweight tent is the only one worth buying, and is never going to be cheap.

COSTS
Once we move on to sleeping bags and tents we are into real money. Think of hiring, of the end-of-season sales, and advertising for good secondhand gear. The prices I give here are only averages. Don't expect to pay more for less, or get much (if any) change from the prices quoted.

```
Sleeping bag (synthetic filling) ..............£50
Tent: lightweight with flysheet ..............£55
Sleeping pad (Karrimor) ...................£2.50
```

You can get down bags like the Blacks Icelandic for about £50 and tents like the YHA Venture for £48.50, but this will, I hope, indicate that camping equipment is not cheap. Think of hiring to start with, until you know what you want.

SAFETY GEAR

You should carry a whistle (six blasts, followed by a minute's silence, then another six blasts etc. is the Distress Signal).

A bivvy bag is light and can be a life-saver if you get weatherbound or have a touch of exposure. A torch and some emergency food is also worth packing up — just in case you bite off more than you can chew. A few extra pounds in weight may be a lifesaver but common sense weighs and costs less.

LONG DISTANCE FOOTPATHS

The first long distance footpath was established — as an idea — just 30 years ago, in 1949. To bring the idea to reality took another 16 years and the first real path, the Pennine Way, only opened in 1965, and has since become the M1 of the Long Distance footpaths. Like the M1 itself, once it was established others followed and there are now, at a rough count, about 25 of them. These are the 'Ways' — the South Downs Way, the Cotswold Way, the Pennine Way, Offa's Dyke, etc., and there are many others of varying length, for no one has yet defined how long a long-distance footpath has to be. Some are not open all along their route, some are not completely 'waymarked', and some are unofficial, and established solely by linking up existing footpaths into a long series of walks. This indeed is the basis of all long distance footpaths with rights-of-way being negotiated or purchased to link up the gaps.

Walking a long-distance footpath is a real challenge and in many ways the culmination of the rambler's activities. Once you are fit and organized, a summer or winter holiday of one or two weeks can accommodate most of the U.K. walks as you can see from the following examples:—

```
Cleveland Way........................ 93 miles
Cotswold Way ....................... 100 miles
Crosses Way ........................ 53 miles
Dales Way .......................... 81 miles
Essex Way .......................... 50 miles
```

Hadrians Way	73 miles
Lyke Wyke Walk	44 miles
North Buckinghamshire Way	30 miles
North Downs Way	60 miles
Offa's Dyke	168 miles
Oxfordshire Way	70 miles
Peakland Way	96 miles
Ridgeway	85 miles
South Downs Way	80 miles
Sandstone Trail	25 miles

This is just a selection but I expect that some of these are new to you. A full list can be obtained from the Ramblers Association (see Chapter 10).

As you can see they offer anything from a long day to three week's walking in all parts of the country — and then there is always France, Spain, Austria and Germany to follow. It would take you a lifetime to walk them all.

PREPARATIONS

The first task when preparing to walk a long distance footpath is to collect all the information you can on the walk and the countryside along its route. Start by writing to The Long Distance Walkers Association, 11 Thorn Bank, Onslow Village, Guildford, Surrey. They know all about the footpaths and can give practical advice. The Countryside Commission, Crescent Place, Cheltenham, Gloucestershire, are also helpful. Get good maps of at least 1:50,000 or 1:25,000 for the mountainous tracks, especially if you intend a winter trip and if the route is not shown, on the map, mark it in.

Then plot accommodation sites, Hotels, Hostels, campsites, villages and study the map for farms, rivers and streams. On the South Downs Way for example, there is very little accommodation in winter, and very little water in summer. Planning is the secret of a successful long-distance walk.

GETTING FIT

To walk a long distance path of say 100 miles, carrying a load of about 30 lbs., you need to be fit. Start by walking up to 15 miles per day, carrying a full pack loaded up to 40 lbs. and always containing all the gear you intend to take. Try and see what you can do without.

CHECKING EQUIPMENT

Before you leave, have all your equipment checked and, if necessary, changed. Check the boots, and have new cleated soles and heels fitted — an essential precaution against slips, especially on grass slopes or icy paths. Calculate food requirements and possibilities for replenishment on the trail. Weight, weight, weight, remember!

COMPANIONS

The right companion for an afternoon's stroll may not prove to be the right one for seven days out on the trail. Try and make shorter trips together first, to shake down your attitudes, agree on such matters as the pace you travel and who does what when you stop. If you can't agree — part.

WALKING FOR FUN

Walking is for fun, of course, but we are talking of people who tend to regard walking as an end in itself. For many people, though, it is a means to an end, and is simply a method of getting out into the wild places to practise some other pastime like photography, bird watching, or botany, perhaps even the study of architecture or archaeology. All these are walking *objectives* and can easily be grafted on to a walker's everyday activities.

WINTER WALKING

In this chapter we have laid down the basics for a progressive series of walking trips which can lead you from the local wood, to the high wild places. Walking is a skill as well as a sport and it takes time and practice to build up the necessary experience. Once you have done so, and not before, consider winter walking, not just for a day but for a long trip.

Even the most crowded footpaths are empty in winter, although not as much as they used to be, for walking is essentially a cold weather activity. The popular view is that it can only be enjoyed in the blazing heat of summer, but such statistics as there are reveal that as many or more walk in the colder seasons.

Winter walking is a more challenging activity than the summer version, and needs to be tackled progressively. Stick to a few short winter rambles before tackling anything major or remote but once tried it is sure to be adopted. Try it and see for yourself.

The secret, if there is a secret, is PREPARATION. Preparation is also part of the fun, and without it much of the pleasure can be lost or is at risk. So plan carefully and plan ahead.

Chapter 7

MAINTENANCE

Walking clothing and camping equipment is, as we have seen, expensive, and this fact alone makes careful maintenance worthwhile, if not essential.

CLOTHING
Walking can be hot work and the trail is often muddy. The mud should be allowed to dry and then brushed off. Regular cleaning will do the clothes less harm than allowing the grit to saw away at the fibres.

Socks or stockings should be washed regularly and never darned. Some people claim to darn neatly, but to my mind a darn is a certain blister. Wash by hand in warm soapy water, not in a machine.

Buttons should be checked and re-sewn before they fall off, and zips can be eased by rubbing with a pencil lead — the graphite will stop them sticking. Don't use oil. Any tears should be neatly stitched.

Wet anoraks, especially if down-filled, need gentle drying in a warm room, and must not be draped over a radiator. MOAC Ltd. have a preparation called *Soppy,* which is very suitable for washing your down sleeping bags and garments.

PROOFING
The proofing on cagoules and windproof smocks can be rubbed away by the rubbing of the pack. Proofing agents can be purchased at most camping shops, but it is always best to consult the manufacturer for his advice on the correct proofing agent for his particular tent or garment.

GAITERS
Scour the mud off, especially from zips and let them dry gently. A wipe with a (very) lightly oiled rag on any buckles, straps or wires, will stop rusting.

BOOTS
Boots need regular cleaning and careful repair. Wash off all the mud the minute you get home. Scrape out mud and stones from the cleats of the sole, and place the boots in a warm room on a newspaper, to dry gently. Do NOT place them in the

fireplace, on a stove, or under a radiator. Once they are dry, put on a good coat of polish or Mars oil, let it dry in, then polish. Some people use dubbin, but current thinking has it that dubbin is bad for the stitches and some manufacturers will refuse to honour the guarantee on dubbined boots. You will get used to the fact that this year's gospel is next year's heresy.

WATERPROOFING

Regular cleaning and repair will help keep your boots water resistant. A preparation by Kiwi called 'Wet-Pruf' also seems useful. If a boot is truly waterproof, it means that you have sealed the pores in the leather, and your feet will sweat uncomfortably, and become very chilly. A little 'Wet-Pruf' on the sides and across the instep is a help, but true waterproofing, even if possible, is not really desirable. Another preparation, Nikwax, is very popular and effective.

SOLE AND HEEL

A good thick sole and heel is essential. They cushion your feet against stony ground, and *worn heels* are a major cause of *slips*, which in turn are the prime cause of walking accidents. Never let the heels wear down.

Have your boots re-soled by a proper boot repairer regularly, and never travel with worn heels. A few climbing nails or 'hobs' of the tri-couni pattern, screwed into the instep is a good idea for winter walking or scrambling, and will give grip on slippery slopes and 'verglas' (ice). Buy heel-crampons if possible.

Fig. 14

SAFETY STRIPS

A strip of reflective tape on your sleeve or rucksack can be a lifesaver on a narrow country lane at night. If it gets worn it becomes useless, so always replace this at the first sign of wear.

STOVES, TORCHES, MATCHES

Rust and damp are the enemy here. Empty out the rucksack, turn it up to let any water drain out, and spread out the contents to dry and air. Replace any expended items, remove the batteries from your torch, and be sure the matches, salt etc. are dry. Keep the matches in a tight container like a film box.

TENTS

Hang them up in a warm place to air and dry before re-folding and re-packing. Straighten and dry any damaged pegs and sand off any rust. Grit and dust should be vacuumed out of the groundsheet. Beware of mildew.

COMPASS

Don't leave the compass lying on top of the T.V. set, by the radio or in the glove compartment of the car. Electrical interference can destroy its magnetic field and give you an incorrect reading. Compasses are precision instruments and must be treated with care.

MAPS

Wind and rain are hard on maps. Dry them flat, fold carefully, using masking tape (on the back) to hold any tears in place and with a soft rubber, erase this weekend's rulings and marks. Never use a hard lead pencil on a map as the marks won't erase.

Repair any tears, and reinforce along the folds with masking tape, never with transparent adhesive tape.

All maintenance should be done as soon as possible after you get home. It is very tempting to have a bath, and collapse contentedly with the papers, but if meanwhile your gear is rotting in the rucksack you are building up trouble for yourself later on.

All the above maintenance takes much less than half an hour, and all maintenance should be done immediately you get back.

The maintenance you do before you set off is called CHECKING — and don't neglect that either!

Chapter 8

PROBLEMS

If you are sensible and let the scope of your activities grow naturally from a basis of experience, your problems will be few. A few, however, are almost inevitable.

BLISTERS

Well-chosen and well-fitting footwear and well-washed socks are the first line of defence against blisters. Well, well, well?

After, say half-an-hour of walking, you may notice a 'hot-spot', the beginnings of a blister, on your toes or heel. Stop at once and investigate. If the rubbing or a reddened patch indicates a 'hot-spot', cut off a piece of *Scholls* 'moleskin' plaster, and cover the spot carefully, being careful not to ruck the plaster when you replace your sock.

If a blister develops, your action depends on whether it has broken or not. If it is intact, cover it with 'Moleskin' and change your socks. Do NOT burst the blister with a needle. It may let the fluid out, but it lets infection in.

If the blister is open, get your scissors and trim off any loose skin. Try and bathe the feet to cool the skin down, and remove any dirt. Replace with a breathable plaster, to let air heal the raw skin, and put on clean socks. In the evening, try and let the air get to the raw spots, as this will help to dry the blisters and stop them stinging. Cleanliness is very important, for septic blisters can be very painful and slow to heal.

SUNBURN AND WINDBURN

Faces unused to fresh air can be flayed by the sun and wind. Drinking hot tea through chapped lips can be a lively experience! For a weekend trip or for the first day or two of a week's holiday, finish the morning wash by rubbing a little cold cream on to the face and hands. A lip salve can stop your lips breaking open.

Beware of sun and wind burn on the neck, where the top of your anorak rubs, for this again can lead to a miserable trip.

EXHAUSTION

If you are unused to walking and carrying a pack, don't be surprised if you get very tired indeed after a few hours on the trail. Heat exhaustion on a humid summer day is due to lack of salt after excessive perspiration, and can usually be cured by drinking lots of water, with a little salt, and cooling off in the shade. Cold exhaustion can be a killer, and is due to lack of food, unsuitable clothing, and over-exertion. If unchecked this leads to hypothermia.

HYPOTHERMIA

Hypothermia occurs in conditions of cold, wind and wet. Look out for the symptoms at such times. It is usually indicated by uncharacteristic behaviour in the victim, and can rapidly lead to a stress situation.

Sullen behaviour, bursts of chatter, falling behind, or stumbling, becoming aggressive and confused speech, are all signs of hypothermia. If someone says "What's got into Alan today?" it may be exhaustion, so let that thought occur to you.

Prevention is the best cure. Start the day with a good breakfast, and wear garments suitable to the weather and the activity. Once signs are noticed STOP AT ONCE. Get the victim out of the wind and get him/her warm. Extra clothing, body warmth from a companion, putting up a tent or windbreak, getting the victim into a sleeping bag — anything to restore body heat and reverse the chilling process which will, if it proceeds, lead to unconsciousness. If the victim becomes unconscious you must get medical help *immediately*.

WIND CHILL

Low temperatures in themselves are no real problem if you are adequately clad, and keep moving. However, if the wind gets up, as can easily happen in cold, frosty weather, then the *effective* temperature is much lower than the true air temperature. At say, $-1°C$ a 20 mile an hour wind gives an *effective temperature much below the true air temperature of $-1°C$,* and that can be lethal if you are not prepared for it. Watch out for wind chill.

WIND CHILL CHART

Wind Speed	Local Temperature (F)			
0	32	23	14	5
5	29	20	10	1
10	18	7	−4	−15
15	13	−1	−13	−25
20	7	−7	−19	−32
30	1	−13	−27	−41

As you can see, the effect of the wind can be dramatic.

FIRST AID

This book forms part of a series and for more information in First Aid out of doors, you should read *'Outdoor First Aid'* (Venture Guide 90p). A knowledge of First Aid is an essential outdoor skill.

TRAFFIC

Cars and people frequently collide on narrow country roads. It happens to adults as well as to children. Always walk facing the oncoming traffic. Carry a torch as soon as the visibility gets poor, and try and wear something white. Shine the torch on yourself as the cars approach, particularly in rainy weather. If *You* can see them don't just assume that *They* can see you.

A few strips of reflective tape on the rucksack, or across the breast pocket of your anorak will be unmistakeable in the headlights of a car and give due warning of your presence. Walkers do get run over, and it is only sensible to take precautions. Reflective armbands are also a very good idea.

WEATHER

Regular weather reports are published in the National Press, broadcast on national and local radio and shown on T.V. Every outdoor-man and woman must obtain regular weather forecasts and update them as often as possible. This is useful at any time, but particularly important in cold weather or in remote areas. The *Spur Book of Weather Lore* is a worthwhile purchase (Venture Guide 90p).

STREAM CROSSINGS

Don't. Many books give bits of advice on methods of crossing streams in spate, but the best advice is to stay out of them.

We are not talking about a rivulet or a little trickle in a meadow. You can splash across those and with laced boots and tight gaiters you won't even get your feet wet, but deep streams and mountain torrents should be avoided. Head upstream until the stream narrows enough to jump across, or you find a bridge or ford.

If you *do* decide to cross (you fool) remove the rucksack and either carry it under one arm or loop on strap lightly over your shoulder so that if you go under you can drop it and come up. Roping-up to a companion while crossing is useful, but it presumes you have a rope. Never follow a stream downhill at night or in fog. Water takes the shortest route off a hill and it will probably lead you over a cliff.

CROSSING GATES AND WALLS

When climbing a gate, go over at the hinged end. There is less risk of bending them like that. Don't jump off the top of a wall if wearing a rucksack. You will be weighing about 25% more than usual and in mid-air you will suddenly realize that you are going to land HARD.

On soft ground you will go sprawling and if you land on a hidden rock or branch it could be nasty.

Never jump *down* from anywhere you can't jump *up!*

FIRES AND SMOKING

Be careful with fires, in everything that has to do with them. Peering into a petrol-fuming rucksack, with a lighted cigarette in your mouth can be one way of losing your eyebrows. Don't start open fires in the countryside and if you do, be sure they are out before you move on. Be careful lighting and filling petrol or paraffin stoves. NEVER START FIRES. Many areas prohibit not only fires but smoking, especially in the height of summer when the woods are like tinder. If a sign says don't smoke, DON'T SMOKE — chew a little gum instead.

Walking is not a dangerous occupation. Indeed a safer and more enjoyable pastime can hardly be imagined. It does remain a fact that your feet can take you far from civilization, where a little snag can become a big problem, so a little common sense and a few precautions are never out of place.

Chapter 9

HOTELS, HOSTELLING AND HOLIDAYS

A walk can begin in a car park, from your front door, from a bus or train station or from a camp site. These points give you considerable choice but it is also possible to combine walking tours with overnight stops in hotels or hostels, which in poor weather can be a considerable advantage.

HOSTELS

Hostelling began in Germany at the turn of the century. The first British hostel opened in 1930, and by April 1931 there were 20. Today there are 256 hostels in England and Wales and a further 150 in Scotland. The Youth Hostels Association has links with similar organizations in over 50 countries and, although the rules vary, they are no longer restricted to the walker or the very young.

Hostels come in all sizes, but basically consist of a fairly simple building with separate dormitories for males and females, each equipped with double tier bunks. They can provide a hot evening meal and packed lunches to order and expect the hostellers to help out with a few simple chores before leaving in the morning.

It is usually necessary to book ahead for there are now 300,000 members of the Y.H.A., and the hostels fill up early, especially at weekends and in the summer. You must have or hire a sheet sleeping bag of the Y.H.A. approved pattern.

COSTS

Hostel charges for the standard grade hostel are currently about £1 per night, and membership of the Y.H.A. currently costs 85p for a young member (5-16 years), and £1.50 for a junior (16-20 years) and £2.50 for a senior (21 plus). Family membership currently costs £5 per year and covers all children under 16 years.

The Y.H.A. has equipment shops and membership centres in London, Manchester and Birmingham and headquarters at 8 St. Stephen's Hill, St. Albans, Herts., AL1 2OY.

HOSTELLING ABROAD

There are over 4,000 Youth Hostels (Auberge de Jeunesse) abroad and membership of the Y.H.A., plus a photograph in your Y.H.A. membership pass, entitles you to use them.

HOTELS

Most hotels and boarding houses in country districts welcome walkers and often arrange walking tours or suggest routes for their guests to follow.

The Holiday Fellowship of 142-144 Great North Way, London NW4 ·1EG (Tel. No: 01-203-3381) has currently seventeen different walking holidays on offer including trips along the South Downs Way and the Cleveland Way.

There are seven National Parks in the U.K. which encourage outdoor tourism. These have marked trails and offer good scope for walking holidays. Details are obtainable from the Countryside Commission, Cheltenham.

The English Tourist Board has a publication entitled *'Outdoor Activity and Sports Holidays'* which gives details of 24 organizations offering walking holidays on the moors and fells, and the Welsh, Scots, Irish and most European Tourist Board Offices have similar publications. They are well worth reading.

HOLIDAYS
Certain routes and countries lend themselves to walking tours. In addition to the organizations listed above, walking holidays are very popular in Germany, Luxembourg, Austria, Italy and France.

France has a local and long-distance footpath network which rivals the U.K. and the *Grande Randonnée* includes such challenging Routes as the pilgrim roads to Compostella (GR 65) and the 250-mile trek up the Alps from the Mediterranean to Lake Geneva (GR 52 and 5).

Holidays in Europe for walkers can be arranged by the Y.H.A., the Ramblers Association, and many private concerns like Waymark Travel.

MOUNTAIN HUTS AND BOTHIES
In most mountain regions the dedicated walker will find a network of tracks leading to climbing huts or 'bothies'. A 'bothy' is a fairly rustic chalet, or barn, often originally built as a shelter for livestock, and now adopted by the climbing or hill-walking fraternity. It is usually necessary to be a member of some mountain activity club in order to use them, although the casual visitor would never be turned away.

Standards of comfort vary from the sparse to the spartan, but there is usually a supply of fuel, a few candles, and perhaps some food. Anything you use you are expected to replace or pay for.

* * *

You will see from this brief survey that the facilities for walkers are abundant, if simple. You will hardly find luxury, but you need never lack a roof over your head. For information on all these and other activities for walkers, let us now look at outdoor publications and organizations.

Chapter 10

INFORMATION, BOOKS, ORGANIZATIONS

If you have come this far and decided that you like walking, there exists a host of organizations, groups, publications and aids to help you further. This is just a few of them.

ORGANIZATIONS

The Ramblers Association
1/4 Crawford Mews,
London W1H 1PT
Tel: 01-262 1477

There are some 400 local rambling clubs affiliated to the Ramblers Association, which has over 30,000 members. You should join the R.A. for two reasons. Firstly, they protect the interests of *all* walkers and secondly, they need your support. The local reference library can give you the address of your local group.

The Backpackers Club,
20 St. Michael's Road,
Tilehurst,
Reading,
Berkshire RG3 4RP

The club for lightweight campers and the solitary walker has over 2,000 members, interested in lightweight camping and walking in wild areas. They are a friendly and very experienced crowd, glad to welcome and help new members.

The Long Distance Footpath Association,
11 Thorn Bank,
Onslow Village,
Guildford,
Surrey.

For advice on all the U.K.'s expanding long distance network, including competitive walking events.

The Youth Hostels Association
Trevelyan House,
St. Albans,
Herts AL1 2DY

The Y.H.A. has branches, equipment shops and bookshops in London, Manchester, Birmingham and Cardiff.

The Camping Club of Great Britain
11 Lower Grosvenor Place,
London SW1

This major organization for campers and ramblers has 80,000 members, publishes a free monthly magazine and has a host of registered camp sites.

PUBLICATIONS

The rambler is well catered for by magazines and books. All the magazines contain good advice and can keep you up-to-date with equipment, current trends, camp sites, advice on gear and facilities. Read at least one of these magazines every month.

'Practical Camper' and *'Camping'* cater for the family and lightweight camper and rambler, and are published every month.

'The Great Outdoors' looks after the backpacker, the walker, and all out-of-door interests, with many interesting feature articles and advice from experienced outdoor people.

'Climber and Rambler' is largely concerned with rock climbing, mountaineering and hilltrekking, but contains useful articles and features for the lowland rambler.

BOOKS

Most public libraries have shelves of hardback books devoted to outdoor skills and activities.

John Hillaby's 'Journey' books (Journey Through Britain; Journey Through Europe etc.), are very enjoyable and now available in paperback. There are others, but few so readable.

Spurbooks' 'Venture Guide' series (this is one of them) and E.P.'s 'Know the Game' books, teach basic outdoor skills, like Map Work, Camping, Cooking etc.

Footpath guides, which give details of walks, the length, where to park, refreshment and degree of difficulty are published by Spurbooks, Gerrard Publications, Dalesman, Moorland, Wainwright, and a host of other local publishers and tourist offices. Many local newspapers give a weekly local walk. They are all worth trying and if written by Footpath groups can show you some wonderful country. Most of the publications are in paperback.

MAPS

O.S. maps are available from many good bookshops, the Y.H.A. branches and most outdoor shops. In case of difficulty you can write for a list of stockists to the Ordnance Survey, Romsey Road, Southampton.

Stanfords of Long Acre, London, have the most comprehensive stock of maps and guides in the South of England, while Austicks in Leeds provide a similar service in the North of the country. If you need something rare, try them.

Stanfords also stock the TOPO guides to the great French footpaths, and maps from the Institut Geographique National Their 903 map 1cm:10km gives all the footpaths and serves as the catalogue for the TOPO guides.

EQUIPMENT STOCKISTS

Throughout this book we have advised you to go to an outdoor equipment shop for all your gear.

The U.K. is well served by outdoor equipment stockists and any new rambler would be well advised to consult his local outdoor shop for advice on his particular needs. The advice is willingly given, and free! To name just a few; *Nevisport* have three branches in Scotland, while *Pindisports* are established in London, Ealing, Bristol and Birmingham.

The *Y.H.A.* has three shops, Scout-Shops several more, and *Blacks* over thirty, with outlets in most major cities. The North and Midlands are particularly well served with good shops.

'Climber and Rambler' carries a list of outdoor shops in every issue and there is sure to be one near you. Apart from their role as stockists and advice centres, most outdoor shops act as a focus for local outdoor activity. If you need a club, an idea, a piece of advice or a companion they can usually help.

HOLIDAYS

An increasing number of companies are offering walking holidays in the U.K. and Europe. The two biggest are Waymark Holidays and Rambler Tours.

INSTRUCTION

If you want to develop your skills under instruction you should write to The National Centre for Mountain Activities, Plas y Brenin, North Wales, for a list of their courses. In Scotland a similar service is offered at Glenmore Lodge, Aviemore, Scotland.

CONCLUSION

This book was written at the suggestion of Ray Jones of the Y.H.A., who said there was a need for some basic advice for walkers. We hope we have provided it. If you, the reader, have any ideas for improvements or suggestions for other books please write and tell us.

Meantime, Good Luck and Good Walking!